Earthquakes

KER THAN

Children's Press®
An Imprint of Scholastic Inc.
New York   Toronto   London   Auckland   Sydney
Mexico City   New Delhi   Hong Kong
Danbury, Connecticut

Content Consultant

K. Shafer Smith, Ph.D.
Associate Professor, Center for Atmosphere Ocean Science
Courant Institute of Mathematical Sciences
New York University
New York, NY

Library of Congress Cataloging-in-Publication Data

Than, Ker, 1980-
  Earthquakes / by Ker Than.
    p. cm. -- (A true book)
  Includes index.
      ISBN-13: 978-0-531-16882-0 (lib. bdg.) 978-0-531-21350-6 (pbk.)
      ISBN-10: 0-531-16882-4 (lib. bdg.) 0-531-21350-1 (pbk.)

1. Earthquakes--Juvenile literature. I. Title. II. Series.

  QE521.3.T43 2009
    551.22--dc22   2008014782

Produced by Weldon Owen Education Inc.

1 2 3 4 5 6 7 8 9 10 R 18 17 16 15 14 13 12 11 10 09

Find the Truth!

Everything you are about to read is true *except* for one of the sentences on this page.

Which one is **TRUE**?

T or F   Earth's surface is broken up into several large pieces like a jigsaw puzzle.

T or F   Scientists can predict exactly when and where earthquakes will strike.

Find the answers in this book.

Contents

THE BIG TRUTH!

The shape of a pagoda resists
damage from earthquakes.

Many buildings are not built
to withstand earthquakes.

CHAPTER 1

Shakes and Shocks

There is one type of natural disaster that is almost impossible to predict and completely impossible to prevent. Earthquakes crumple roads and topple buildings. They hurl loose objects through the air and even start fires. Scientists know what causes the earth to shake. But they often can't predict quakes in time to keep people safe.

Collapsing buildings, flying objects, and people falling cause most earthquake injuries.

The Big One

Most people who live in the state of California can expect to experience at least one earthquake during their lifetime. Most quakes are mild. However, some have caused great death and destruction.

In the early morning of April 18, 1906, the ground in the San Francisco Bay Area shook for about 45 seconds. The shaking was so strong that it was felt from Oregon to Los Angeles and as far inland as central Nevada.

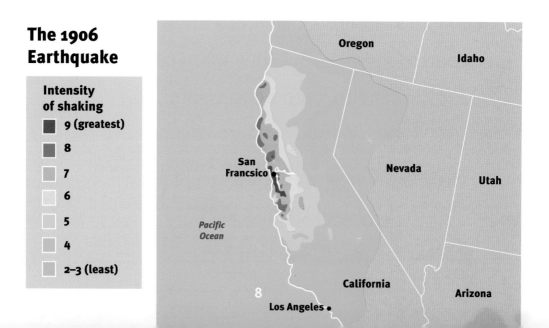

The 1906 Earthquake

Intensity of shaking
- 9 (greatest)
- 8
- 7
- 6
- 5
- 4
- 2–3 (least)

Oregon

Idaho

San Francsico

Nevada

Utah

Pacific Ocean

California

Arizona

Los Angeles

The Effects

In the city of San Francisco, streets rippled like a stormy sea. The ground ruptured. Buildings collapsed, trapping people beneath the rubble.

Gas from cracked gas pipes sparked blazes that burned for three days and nights. In an effort to stop the spread of the blaze, firefighters used dynamite to blow up buildings in its path. However, they succeeded only in sparking new fires.

As much as 90 percent of the damage in San Francisco was from fires.

Because the water supply was damaged in the quake, little could be done to stop the fires.

9

The Aftermath

The 1906 San Francisco earthquake and fires caused billions of dollars in damage, in today's dollars. Nearly 30,000 buildings were destroyed. Half the people in the city were left homeless. Officially, about 500 people were listed as killed. New research suggests an actual death toll as high as 3,000. It was one of the worst natural disasters in U.S. history.

After the quake, city officials rushed to rebuild in time for the 1915 world's fair. At the time, there was still little knowledge about earthquake safety. Many new buildings were no safer than the old ones.

However, within days of the 1906 quake, California's governor gathered a team of **geologists** to study earthquakes. This began a new era of earthquake research. The more scientists learn about earthquakes, the more they can protect people from them.

The 1906 California earthquake was one of the first major natural disasters to be recorded by photography.

This rift valley is in Thingvellir (THEENG-vetl-ir), Iceland. It lies above the fault where two enormous tectonic plates are slowly moving apart.

CHAPTER 2

On Shaky Ground

The ground beneath your feet might look as if it is standing still. However, that is an illusion. Earth's surface, or **crust**, is made up of many huge slabs called **tectonic plates**. These slabs fit together like pieces of a jigsaw puzzle. However, unlike puzzle pieces, they are in constant motion.

Tectonic plates move less than 3 inches (7 centimeters) per year.

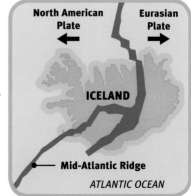

North American Plate ←

Eurasian Plate →

ICELAND

Mid-Atlantic Ridge

ATLANTIC OCEAN

Under the Surface

Tectonic plates float on a layer of hot, soft rock. Some neighboring plates slide past one another. Others move apart or slowly crash together, with one plate sliding under the other. Plates move slowly. They move only at about the same rate as your fingernails grow!

The Andes Mountains of South America formed where the Nazca Plate collides with the South American Plate.

Plates of the World

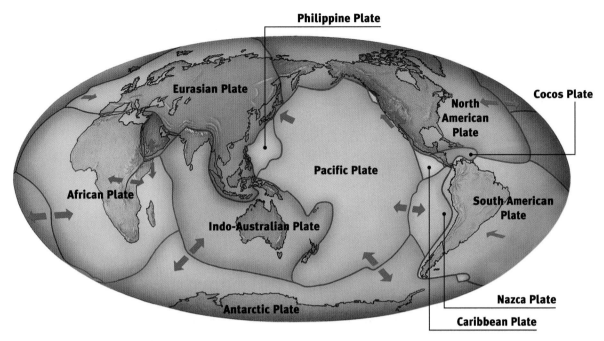

The place where the edges of two tectonic plates meet is called a **fault**. Sometimes two plates get caught on one another along a fault. When this happens, **friction** causes tremendous pressures to build up inside the plates. Tectonic plates that get stuck together eventually tug free in sudden movements called **fault slips**.

Slips and Shocks

Fault slips can release enormous amounts of energy. The released energy travels through Earth as **seismic waves**. These waves can break even the hardest rock. When seismic waves reach Earth's surface, they make the ground shake and an earthquake occurs.

The underground location where the earthquake starts is called the hypocenter. The epicenter is the point on Earth's surface directly above the hypocenter. This is where seismic waves are strongest.

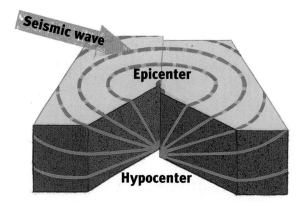

The seismic waves lose strength as they spread away from the epicenter of an earthquake.

Detector Dragon

Nearly 2,000 years ago, a Chinese astronomer named Zhang Heng (jahng-huhng) invented the world's first earthquake detector. It was a large bronze pot with dragon heads on it. Each dragon had a metal ball in its mouth. When the ground shook, one or more balls fell into the mouth of a metal toad below. The dragon with the empty mouth pointed in the direction of the earthquake. Heng's invention could detect an earthquake more than 370 miles (600 kilometers) away.

Faults and Friction

Faults between tectonic plates can be very large. Some extend for hundreds of miles. The San Andreas Fault in western North America is a large fault. Other well-known large faults are the Nojima Fault in Japan and the North Anatolian Fault in Turkey.

Not all faults are large, however. Any crack between shifting layers of rock is considered a fault. Small faults can create **fault lines** in rock faces, riverbanks, and cliffs. Like the large, deep faults that cause earthquakes, small faults also generate friction that may lead to slippage.

In Japan, there are hundreds of faults the size of the Nojima Fault.

In central Japan, a fault line from the Nojima Fault cuts a clear path through terraced rice fields.

Earthquake Clusters

Earthquakes usually occur in clusters. The most powerful earthquake in a cluster is called the mainshock. Any ground shaking before it is called a foreshock. A quake that occurs after it is called an aftershock. Aftershocks are usually smaller movements in the plate that caused the initial quake. An aftershock can occur decades after a mainshock. Some foreshocks and aftershocks are too weak for people to feel.

The patterns in this California rock show how the ground has moved.

Making Quakes

Occasionally, earthquakes result from human activity. Damming rivers creates new bodies of water. This can put a huge amount of pressure on underground faults. Mining for coal and pumping up oil also change the pressure on a fault and can set off quakes.

Human-made quakes are usually mild – but not always. When people change the pressure on a major fault, they could set off a serious quake.

There are thousands of oil fields in Texas. However, no more than a few small earthquakes have occurred, at only a few of these sites.

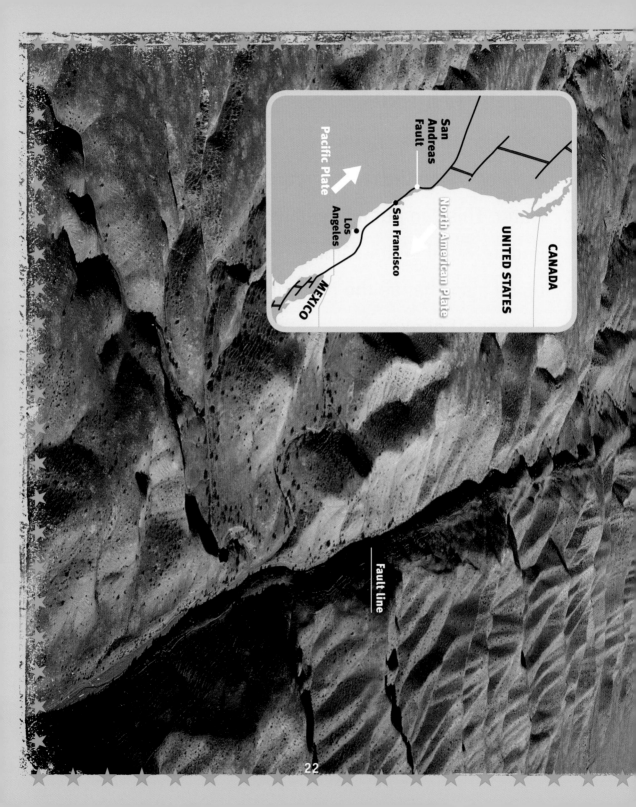

San
Andreas
Fault

Pacific Plate

Los
Angeles

San Francisco

North American Plate

UNITED STATES

CANADA

MEXICO

Fault line

Famous Fault

The San Andreas Fault is about 600 miles (970 kilometers) long. It cuts vertically through California. Two tectonic plates moving slowly in opposite directions formed the fault. For long periods, the plate edges strain to pass each other. An earthquake occurs when the mounting pressure between the plates finally leads to a fault slip. A fault line above the San Andreas Fault can be seen as a valley-like scar running through the Carrizo Plain in California.

Two Plates

For about 28 million years, the Pacific Plate has been moving northwest at an average of 2 inches (5 centimeters) per year. The North American Plate has been moving southeast at the same rate.

Two Cities

San Francisco sits along the San Andreas Fault, on the North American Plate. The city of Los Angeles sits near the fault on the Pacific Plate. Scientists estimate that in about 15 million years, the two cities could be next to each other!

Carrizo Plain

In 1989, another major earthquake struck the San Francisco Bay Area. The Cypress Street freeway in Oakland, California, collapsed.

CHAPTER 3

Risk and Rescue

Earthquakes can happen anywhere and at any time. However, they strike some parts of Earth more often than others. There are many large cities in high-risk zones. As more people move into cities in the coming years, more people may be at risk. Scientists, city planners, engineers, and government officials all contribute to earthquake preparations in risk zones.

It took 9 years and $1.2 billion to rebuild the Cypress Street freeway.

Hotspots

About 80 percent of Earth's largest earthquakes occur near the Ring of Fire. This horseshoe-shaped region in the Pacific Ocean is where many tectonic plates meet. It includes the eastern edge of Asia and the western coasts of North America and South America. The Ring of Fire is also dotted with volcanoes.

Some of the world's biggest and fastest-growing cities, such as Tokyo and Mexico City, are located along the Ring of Fire.

The Ring of Fire

ASIA

NORTH AMERICA

•Tokyo
Japan

•Mexico City

Philippines

Pacific Ocean

Indian Ocean

SOUTH

AUSTRALIA

KEY
▲ Active volcano

Inside the Ring

The underground movements that create earthquakes can also set off volcanoes. Quakes in the Ring of Fire often occur just before volcanic eruptions. Quakes preceded the colossal 1991 eruption of Mount Pinatubo, in the Philippines.

Ocean earthquakes in the Ring of Fire can trigger **tsunamis**. These giant waves can cause great destruction when they reach land.

A series of quakes shook the state of Washington in the weeks before the 1980 explosion of Mount St. Helens.

Killer Quake

Wherever major fault lines are located, earthquakes can take place. On May 12, 2008, a massive quake rocked Sichuan (sich-wahn) province in China. More than 60,000 people were killed and about 200,000 were injured. Buildings swayed in Beijing, 1,000 miles (1,600 kilometers) from the epicenter.

The earthquake in China left millions of people homeless. It was the worst quake to hit China in 32 years.

CHINA Beijing

Epicenter

28

Animal Alert

Do animals have a "sixth sense" for earthquakes? Some scientists think that animals may sense weak tremors before a quake. Other scientists think that they may sense electrical signals set off by the shifting of underground rocks. People reported that some animals behaved strangely before the May 2008 earthquake in China. Elephants swung their trunks wildly. Peacocks screeched. Some pandas dropped the bamboo they were eating and started marching around.

Saving Lives

In the middle of the tragedy in China, there were stories of heroic rescue. One infant was found alive, cradled in her dead mother's arms. She had been shielded by her mother's body. A pregnant woman was rescued after being buried for 50 hours under 18 feet (6 meters) of rubble. A few weeks later, she gave birth to a healthy daughter.

The woman named her new baby daughter Ai (love), out of gratitude to all those who helped rescue her.

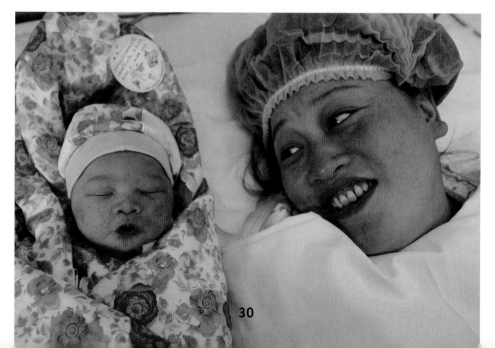

Rescue dogs are trained to move on unstable surfaces and search in tight spaces.

Rescue Dogs

With their keen sense of smell, rescue dogs can help locate people under masses of rubble after earthquakes. After the 1985 earthquake in Mexico City, rescue dogs found eight survivors within five days. Their success made the work of four-legged rescue workers famous around the world. Rescue dogs from many different countries also helped find survivors in China in 2008.

In December 2004, an earthquake (yellow star), shook the Indian Ocean off Sumatra. The seismic waves (white rings) triggered a huge tsunami.

CHAPTER 4

Studying Quakes

Earthquakes have fascinated people for thousands of years. The ancient Greeks believed they were caused by winds rushing out from caves inside Earth. Modern scientists know more about what causes them, but there is still much to learn. By monitoring earthquakes right where they happen, scientists hope to discover how to predict them.

The 2004 Indian Ocean earthquake lasted nearly 10 minutes—the longest on record!

Out of the Wreckage

After the 1906 California earthquake, people could no longer ignore the problem of earthquakes. The team of experts who investigated the 1906 quake were the first to link earthquakes to fault movement. They mapped the entire length of the San Andreas Fault.

Today, scientists around the world observe faults before, during, and after earthquakes. This helps them predict how these faults may behave in the future. They learn more about how much force it takes to create an earthquake, and how large that quake is likely to be.

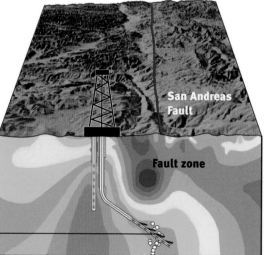

San Andreas Fault

Fault zone

SAFOD instruments lie more than a mile underground. They send data up to scientists.

San Andreas Fault Observatory at Depth (SAFOD)

Recording Earthquakes

Scientists who study earthquakes are called **seismologists** (size-MAH-luh-jists). They record and measure the effects of an earthquake's seismic waves. A device called a seismograph, or seismometer (size-MAH-muh-tur), records movements of the ground.

A basic seismograph consists of a pen suspended over a roll of paper. As the roll turns, the pen traces a line on the paper. Ground movements make the pen trace a zigzag pattern.

Scientists study the zigzag lines created by seismographs. The size of the zigzag helps scientists measure a quake and locate its epicenter.

35

Measuring Earthquakes

Seismologists rate the **magnitude**, or size, of an earthquake by the amount of ground motion it causes. An earthquake is assigned a magnitude number based on seismographic recordings. Magnitudes are based on a system called the Richter scale. The scale is named for the seismologist who invented it. Each number on the Richter scale represents ground motion 10 times stronger than the number before it.

Seismology Time Line

1880
Englishman John Milne invents the seismograph on which modern seismographs are based.

1935
American scientist Charles Richter invents the Richter scale.

A quake of magnitude 3 is 10 times stronger than one of magnitude 2. A quake of magnitude 6 or higher can cause serious damage.

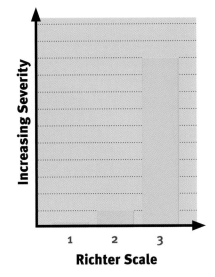

The strongest quake on record measured 9.5. It caused giant ocean waves as far as 6,000 miles (10,000 kilometers) away. At the low end of the Richter scale, people may not even be aware that the ground is shaking.

1977

The U.S. government establishes the National Earthquake Hazards Reduction Program (NEHRP).

2004

The first satellite for earthquake study is launched. It records changes in space that result from tremors.

In Japan, children take part in
regular earthquake safety drills.

CHAPTER 5

Be Prepared

There are some things you can do to protect yourself during a quake. Indoors, you can drop to the floor and get under a desk or sturdy table. Cover your head with one arm and hold on with the other. Outdoors, first move away from buildings, trees, and power lines. Then drop to the ground and cover your head with your arm.

← Japan has more earthquakes than any other country in the world.

Building for Quakes

In cities where earthquakes occur often, some buildings are constructed with quake safety in mind. They have deep foundations and strong, flexible frames. They are designed to absorb vibrations without falling. Sometimes special seismic joints are used. These allow the building to sway slightly.

This house in Berkeley, California, is claimed to be the safest house in the world. Its unusual design absorbs shaking. Its building materials resist fire and water.

Engineers are now also developing "smart buildings." These structures have sensors that will automatically activate special systems during an earthquake. One system uses a kind of shock absorber similar to those in a car. Another system shifts weights on the roof of a building. This counteracts the force of the quake. More systems to reduce damage are being developed.

The Transamerica Pyramid in San Francisco is built to absorb shock waves and resist shaking.

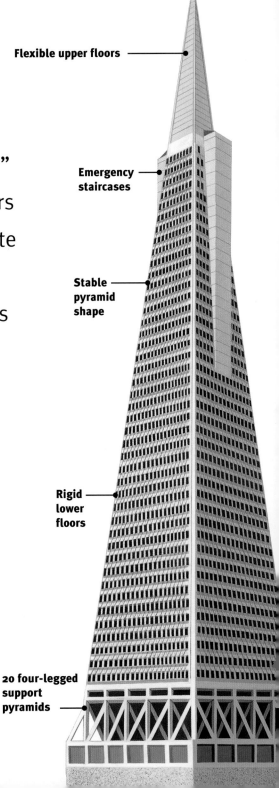

Flexible upper floors

Emergency staircases

Stable pyramid shape

Rigid lower floors

20 four-legged support pyramids

41

Looking Ahead

Earthquakes are difficult to predict. The fault slips that cause them occur far below the surface of Earth. At best, today's scientists can only estimate the chances that a major earthquake will strike a certain region. Technology is constantly improving, however. More accurate predictions in the future may make powerful earthquakes less deadly. ★

The Demeter satellite measures changes in Earth's magnetic field, which may signal an earthquake.

True Statistics

Deaths from one earthquake in China in 1556:
About 830,000

Earthquakes with magnitudes of 2.9 or lower
per year: About 1,300,000

Earthquakes with magnitudes of 8 or higher
per year: About 1

Magnitude of the largest earthquake on record:
9.5 (Chile, 1960)

Magnitude of the largest United States earthquake
on record: 9.2 (Alaska, 1964)

Speed of the fastest seismic waves:
225 miles (360 kilometers) per hour

Did you find the truth?

T Earth's surface is broken up into several large pieces like a jigsaw puzzle.

F Scientists can predict exactly when and where earthquakes will strike.

Resources

Books

Gardner, Robert. *Earth-Shaking Science Projects About Planet Earth.* Berkeley Heights, NJ: Enslow, 2008.

Prokos, Anna. *Earthquakes.* Pleasantville, NY: Gareth Stevens Publishing, 2009.

Scholastic Books. *Our Changing Planet: How Volcanoes, Earthquakes, Tsunamis, and Weather Shape Our Planet.* New York: Scholastic, Inc., 1996.

Stille, Darlene R. *Great Shakes: The Science of Earthquakes.* Mankato, MN: Compass Point Books, 2009.

Trueit, Trudi Strain. *Earthquakes.* New York: Franklin Watts, 2003.

van Rose, Susanna. *Volcano and Earthquake* (Eyewitness Books). New York: DK Children, 2008.

Woods, Michael and Woods, Mary B. *Earthquakes* (Disasters Up Close). Minneapolis, MN: Lerner Publications, 2007.

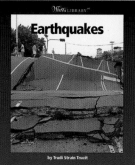

Organizations and Web Sites

Earthquakes for Kids

www.earthquake.usgs.gov/learning/kids/
Learn about earthquakes with games, experiments, and video clips.

FEMA for Kids: Disaster Connection

www.fema.gov/kids/quake.htm
A Web site with a mixture of science and fun activities relating to earthquakes.

The Virtual Museum of the City of San Francisco

www.sfmuseum.net/1906/ew8.html
Read an exciting firsthand account of the great San Francisco earthquake of 1906.

Places to Visit

ShakeZone: The Fingerprints Youth Museum

123 S. Carmalita St.
Hemet, CA 92543
(951) 765 1223
http://fingerprintsmuseum.com/shakezone.html
Interactive displays make earthquakes come alive at the ShakeZone.

The Big One: Burke Museum of Natural History and Culture

Mark R. Hand
Traveling Exhibits Coordinator
(206) 616 0268
www.washington.edu/burkemuseum/exhibits/traveling_bigone.php
Explore "earthquake country" with this traveling exhibition.

Important Words

crust – the hard, outer layer of Earth

fault – a break in Earth's crust produced by the shifting of plates in different directions

fault line – the line formed along the surface of the ground by a fault

fault slip – the sudden shifting of tectonic plates that causes earthquakes

friction – the force that slows down an object whenever it touches something else, such as a surface

geologist – a scientist who studies the structure of Earth, including its rocks, minerals, and soil

magnitude – a measure of how much energy an earthquake releases

seismic wave – a wave of energy caused by the sudden shifting of tectonic plates. Seismic waves travel through Earth and make the ground shake.

seismologist (size-MAHL-uh-jist) – a scientist who studies seismic waves from earthquakes, explosions, or other forces

tectonic plate – one of the large slabs of rock that make up Earth's outer crust

tsunami (tsoo-NAH-mee) – a giant ocean wave caused by an underwater earthquake or a volcanic eruption

Index

About the Author

Ker Than is a science writer living in New York City. He has a master's degree from New York University's Science, Health, and Environmental Reporting Program. Before becoming a freelancer, Ker was a staff writer at the science news Web sites LiveScience.com and Space.com, where he wrote about earthquakes, dinosaurs, black holes, and other interesting things. His Web site is www.kerthan.com.

PHOTOGRAPHS: AAP Image: AP/Greg Baker (p. 30); Big Stock Photo: ©Ramon Purcell (p. 29); Caltech (Charles Richter, p. 36); ©CNES/ill.David Ducros, 2003 (satellite, p. 37; p. 42); FEMA: Federal Emergency Management Agency (p. 3); Getty Images (p. 17; p. 28; p. 32; p. 35); iStockphoto.com (©Andrew Penner, p. 21; ©Carol Oostman, p. 20; ©Fenykepez, p. 14; ©James Benet, seismograph machine, p. 5, seismograph printout, p. 36; ©Jim Parkin, back cover; ©Yali Shi, pagoda, p. 5); NEHRP: National Earthquake Hazards Reduction Program (NEHRP logo, p. 37); Photodisc (p. 27); Photolibrary (p. 9; p. 11; pp. 22–24; p. 40); PhotoNewZealand/Marka (p. 12); Tranz (Corbis, p. 6; p. 19; Reuters, cover; p. 31; p. 38)

The publisher would like to thank Thibéry Cussac of CNES for supplying the satellite illustrations on pages 37 and 42, and also Linda Bustos of Caltech for the photo of Charles Richter on page 36.